Love to you, Margaret
from
Mom & Dad
July, 1997.

Bruce Fenton
26 June '97

SANCTUARY

HALIFAX'S PARKS
& PUBLIC GARDENS

BRUCE ARMSTRONG AND JOHN DAVIS

NIMBUS
PUBLISHING LTD

Nimbus Publishing Limited
P.O. Box 9301, Station A
Halifax, Nova Scotia B3K 5N5
(902) 455-4286

Design: Arthur B. Carter, Halifax
Printed and bound in Hong Kong
by Everbest Printing Co. Ltd.

Canadian Cataloguing in Publication Data
Armstrong, Bruce.
Sanctuary
ISBN 1-55109-150-X
1. Gardens—Nova Scotia—Halifax. 2. Parks—Nova Scotia—Halifax. I. Davis, John, 1950-. II. Title.
SB466.C22H2 1996   712'.5'09716225   C95-950290-4

Front cover: Summer evening in the Public Gardens.
Back cover: Northern Red Oak in fall, Point Pleasant Park.
Title page: Autumn day, Public Gardens.

CONTENTS

INTRODUCTION 4

THE PUBLIC GARDENS 6

FLEMING PARK 30

HEMLOCK RAVINE 48

POINT PLEASANT PARK 64

INTRODUCTION

The Halifax Public Gardens and the large woodland parks are no ordinary places. More than ever, I am convinced that Halifax is unique among other Canadian cities, with so many expansive parks dispersed throughout an urban area. Each park echoes the past, has its own distinctive charm. Each one is a verdant sanctuary within an urban sprawl, situated by happenstance of history. And most importantly, all retreats are easily accessible within or from the city—a walk, jog, drive, or bus ride, and the soul is rejuvenated.

In the centre of the peninsula that makes up urban Halifax are what have been called "the finest Victorian public gardens in North America." Situated downtown on Spring Garden Road next to condos and shops, the Public Gardens take up an entire city block. The gardens have been sculpted using a formal design to display sumptuous arrangements of imported and domestic trees, shrubs, and flowers. There are classical statues, elaborate fountains, winding pathways, crowded duck ponds, and an ornate wooden bandstand. The gardens are open from spring until late autumn; by ecological necessity, they are dormant during winter.

Fleming Park sits in the western quadrant of the mainland and is located along the scenic Northwest Arm, a peaceful tidal inlet that is popular for sailing and boating. Rising 200 feet in the air, the granite and ironstone Dingle Tower oversees the Northwest Arm and four distinct natural habitats in the park. Gentle rolling hills and leafy dells around the large Frog Pond set the pace for visitors.

In the northern quadrant, along the Bedford Basin shore, a rotunda stands as the only remaining structure of a romantic estate built in 1794 by Prince Edward the Duke of Kent for his companion and lover, Julie St. Laurent. Inland and up the hill opposite the rotunda is Hemlock Ravine, a paradise for birds and wilderness enough for deer. The lovers held soirees and concerts at their lavish country getaway, which had twining woodland paths, temples, pagodas, and secret grottos. The forested ravine, full of wonders and mystery, has since been expanded into a 200-acre ecological site, where 300-year-old hemlocks continue to flourish.

Deep in the south end of the city, overlooking the mouth of Halifax Harbour, is Point Pleasant Park. This popular retreat is a sea-girt forest with serpentine roads, twisting bridle paths, what were once broad carriage drives, and a sandy beach. In late September, Point Pleasant is radiant with autumn hues. The clean smell of pines in concert with the sounds emanating from the trees and the sea close by stir the senses, soothe the spirit.

Haligonians are fortunate, for the local gardens and parks are lovingly tended. These places are gifts, thanks to those in the past who were not only generous but who recognized "the needs of the soul for retreat," and to those today who help to protect and maintain the full glory of these sanctuaries.

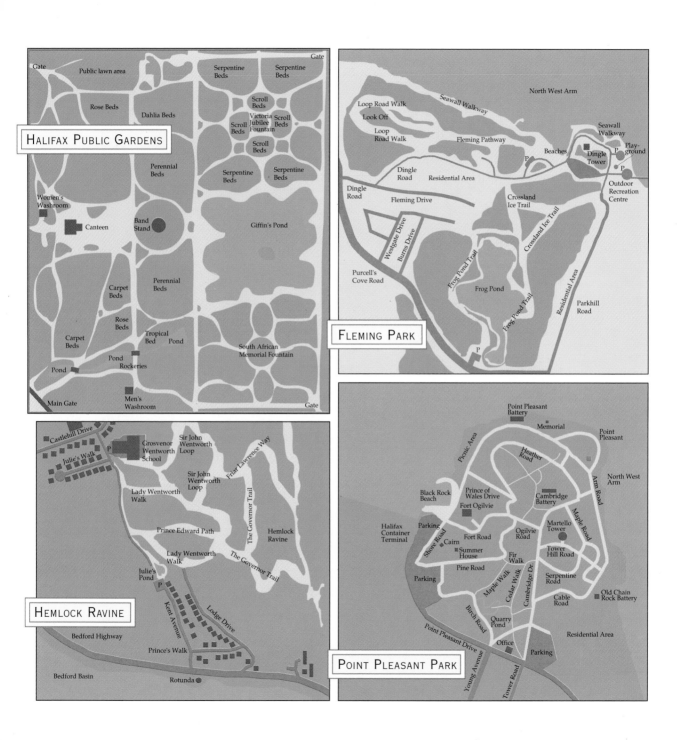

HALIFAX PUBLIC GARDENS

Gate

Public lawn area

Serpentine Beds

Serpentine Beds

Rose Beds

Dahlia Beds

Scroll Beds

Victoria Jubilee Fountain

Scroll Beds

Scroll Beds

Scroll Beds

Gate

Perennial Beds

Serpentine Beds

Serpentine Beds

Women's Washroom

Canteen

Band Stand

Giffin's Pond

Carpet Beds

Perennial Beds

Rose Beds

Tropical Bed

Pond

Carpet Beds

Pond Rockeries

Pond

South African Memorial Fountain

Main Gate

Men's Washroom

Gate

FLEMING PARK

North West Arm

Loop Road Walk

Seawall Walkway

Look Off

Loop Road Walk

Fleming Pathway

Seawall Walkway

Beaches

Dingle Tower

Playground

Dingle Road

Residential Area

P

Dingle Road

Fleming Drive

Crossland Ice Trail

Outdoor Recreation Centre

Westgate Drive

Burns Drive

Crossland Ice Trail

Purcell's Cove Road

Frog Pond Trail

Frog Pond

Residential Area

Parkhill Road

Frog Pond Trail

P

HEMLOCK RAVINE

Castlehill Drive

P

Grosvenor Wentworth School

Sir John Wentworth Loop

Julie's Walk

Sir John Wentworth Loop

Friar Lawrence Way

Lady Wentworth Walk

The Governor Trail

Prince Edward Path

Hemlock Ravine

Lady Wentworth Walk

The Governor Trail

Julie's Pond

P

Kent Avenue

Lodge Drive

Bedford Highway

Prince's Walk

Bedford Basin

Rotunda

POINT PLEASANT PARK

Point Pleasant Battery

Memorial

Point Pleasant

Picnic Area

Heather Road

North West Arm

Black Rock Beach

Prince of Wales Drive

Fort Ogilvie

Cambridge Battery

Arm Road

Halifax Container Terminal

Parking

Shore Road

Cairn

Fort Road

Summer House

Ogilvie Road

Martello Tower

Maple Road

Fir Walk

Tower Hill Road

Parking

Pine Road

Maple Walk

Cedar Walk

Cambridge Dr.

Serpentine Road

Old Chain Rock Battery

Cable Road

Birch Road

Quarry Pond

Point Pleasant Drive

Office

Parking

Residential Area

Young Avenue

Tower Road

Wrought-iron gates at the main entrance of the
Public Gardens were shipped from Scotland in 1890.

THE PUBLIC GARDENS

A cool smell of foliage and the scent of flowers fills the air by the wide stretch of sidewalk bordering the gardens. It is a morning in June. My backpack is crammed with notebooks, lunch, and a small pair of field glasses. Through the wrought-iron fence and beyond some shrubbery, there is a blaze of startling red and yellow. The trees in the park are rife with singing colour.

"The green trees when I saw them first through one of the gates transported and ravished me; their sweetness and unusual beauty made my heart to leap, and almost mad with ecstasy, they were such strange and wonderful things." The English writer Thomas Traherne was referring to other gardens. Nevertheless, many share his passion for trees—great green reservoirs of life, as naturalist John Hay calls them. I walk through the heavy swinging gate of this leafy retreat, which holds imported species from all over the world. Here, in the green and flowery heart of an old port city full of trees, are what have been called the finest Victorian public gardens in North America.

Seated on a bench under a chestnut tree, I drink my morning coffee. Over a hundred years ago the park benches were crowded with pipe-puffing, bold young men. Women were seldom offered a seat, but at least the park was a refuge for their long skirts from expectorated pools of chewing tobacco on every street corner. Today, office workers step briskly along the garden paths clutching plastic mugs of "java" to get them through the morning. The gardeners are at work; the pram pushers are out.

If ever a visitor requested some background on these 16-acre gardens my reply would be: "From boggy dumpsite and gallows ground to a fragrant midsummer dream. "Private gardens for public showing, at a nominal fee, existed in Halifax as long ago as the late 1700s. It was Joseph Howe, the great reform politician, who, in his paper the *Novascotian*, carried the initial report of the Nova Scotia Horticultural Society in 1836. Through his paper Howe continually encouraged the building of a public garden, not only for the gentry but especially for the labouring classes who had no recourse to country retreats. Victorian city dwellers had the same desires to have nature retreats as we have today: a place to escape from noise and pollution; a place of natural beauty to replenish the soul; a place of serenity wherein to mix with others in the open air.

With the Victorian era came the Industrial Revolution and the creators of great English gardens. In 1844 Joseph Paxton's Birkenhead near Liverpool, England, was the first park built on land set aside for public use. His ideas of landscaping and gardening design were carried to America. There it flourished under artists like Frederick Law Olmstead, chief designer of Central Park in New York City.

In Halifax, Griffin's Pond and surrounding swampy wasteland on a part of the Commons were being transformed. In 1866, under alderman John McCulloch, this unpleasant dumping ground—the setting for murderer Griffin's hanging—was planted with trees and flowers, and crushed stone paths were laid out. A succeeding group of aldermen with more prosaic tastes had the area planted in corn. But the dream was not lost. Another planting took place, a fountain vase was donated, and soon the Public Gardens became a reality. The Horticultural Society chose Richard Power as superintendent in 1872. He had been the foreman of the Duke of Devonshire's estate in Ireland, trained with Paxton, and was familiar with Olmstead's work in Central Park. It was Power's formal Victorian garden design that made the Public Gardens so well known in North America by the turn of the century. Today, the design remains the same, but the ornate greenhouses have disappeared.

The sun has dried the early morning dew. Pigeons are doing their dance, cooing and courting, as their rainbow collars reflect the light. I toss out a handful of bread crumbs. Pigeons vie with sparrows, starlings, and ducks for offerings; the little birds dodge in and out. Male pigeons

*The 19th century bandstand, around which people
and ducks gather on a hazy, summer afternoon.*

One of the two bridges that span the former Freshwater Brook, a stream
that meanders down from the North Commons where cows
once grazed along its banks, to lose itself in the large duck pond.

strut and twirl in endless courtship. Descendants of the wild rock dove—
a bird more at home on cliffy ledges—these semi-tame and gentle city
pigeons nest on buildings near transoms and ventilators. Natural predators are absent, they multiply freely.

High-pitched squeals come from a nearby hillock shaded by rare
sycamore maples. Children climb up the knoll and, shrieking, roll down
its grassy banks. This spot seems equally cheerful in early spring, which
begins when from the street, you can see around this little hill bright
crocuses pushing up through the cold earth. One has a feeling of antici-
pation and relief, much like Coleridge in his poem of spring flowers and
late frost: "Grief melts away/ Like snow in May,/ As if there were no
such cold thing…." Soon the garden gates, locked all winter, will be open.

But this is June. I munch my sandwich. Starlings hop in and out of the
wire trash container. These iridescent scavengers are much-maligned
birds. "Pests!" farmers say. "No charisma!" others complain. Their charm,
for me, is in their song. They can mimic the calls of other birds and their
long songs are punctuated with chuckles, rattles, clicks, whistles, trills,
and squeaks—a veritable one-bird band. There are many in the gardens.

The morning now blossoms into noon. The sky is flooded with light
and I begin my lazy stroll. This is a romantic park, created during a
romantic era and therein lies its profound charm. The great walls of trees
and dense shrubbery help to keep out the street view and absorb the din
of daily traffic and commerce. The paths meander; there is delight around
each bend in the leafy bowers and the long generous stretches of lawn.
All this provides a feeling of unspoiled pastoral spaciousness, an illusion
of infinity, of eternal Eden.

Layers of rich topsoil have made these gardens. These layers are new.
There exists but a metre of earth covering the slate and siltstone bedrock
beneath Halifax—rock formed millions of years ago. The superintend-
ents, with their skill and devotion over the years, have kept this "highly
managed ecosystem" true to Richard Power's vision. His son and grand-
son would follow in his footsteps, and Power was still gardening a year
before his death at the age of ninety-three.

A summer evening in the Public Gardens
provides sanctuary from the daytime routine.

The path I take wanders through a grove of trees. Here are yellow and European birch, false cypress, northern red oak, and bay-leaved willow. Within the grove a miniature pond offers quiet refuge for birdlife, and across the path is a stone grotto drinking fountain designed in neogothic style, built over a natural spring during the last century.

"How assured, and how easy to love it is!" wrote Colette about the rose. "Every painter's brush has painted it and will go on painting it." Roses seem to be everywhere. Many heritage roses are featured. These are the old fashioned varieties, heavily scented and a joy to the nose. I lean close to the fragrant bushes. From unopened bud, to sensuous blossom, to fallen, delicate, curled petals, the rose remains seductive and ravishing to the very end.

Past the conifer cluster of Austrian and long-leaf pines, the Colorado blue spruce, and California incense cedar tree. Past the London plane tree—a hybrid of the Oriental and London plane—with its piebald trunk that sheds its outer bark annually. Past the prickly Devil's Walking Stick and on to the public lawn area. I love this stretch of grass, which began long ago as a simple vegetable garden. In 1871 the first public lawn-tennis court in Canada was laid out here. Later it served as an archery and croquet ground. "To sit in the shade on a fine day," wrote Jane Austen, "and look upon verdure is the most perfect refreshment." Here, children play, adults gossip, read books, or play chess.

On the west, north, and east sides and through the centre of the gardens are paths bordered with linden and Scotch elms. Whenever I look down these long passages of glorious shady branches, the ever-stretching corridor of tall trees, the vaulted aisles appear timeless—and I feel imbued with a sense of peace. There is an old saying: "When the leaves of elms are just as big as a mouse's ears, but no smaller, mind, and not a shade bigger, then, *then*, is the time for love!" Strolling couples put their arms around each other; these paths are lovers' walks.

Across Summer Street, opposite the northwest gate, is the tree-lined Camp Hill Cemetery, filled with ancient tombstones. Do these memorials name once ardent visitors to the gardens? Perhaps their ghosts move in the summer air in these green rooms of foliage and flower.

A Monarch butterfly, having wintered in Mexico,
takes a well deserved rest on a Jerusalem artichoke.

Victorians loved gilding the lily, as they say, and in their gardens they added a fillip to nature with the discreet use of statues, bird baths, and urns. The "nymph fountain" is a splendid example of Victorian garden design. A couple gazes at the classic elegance of the fountain erected in 1897 to commemorate Queen Victoria's Diamond Jubilee. Egeria, the mythological nymph carrying an urn, stands on top of the large basin from which the water falls. Some children shout with delight at the four bucking water babies riding dolphins. Coaxed by parents, the youngsters toss coins into the fountain for good luck. Around the fountain are trees and bushes such as the Japanese katsura, with flowering crab, laburnum, and tree lilac. There are scroll beds of flowers, and twisting their way across the lawn are serpentine plantings aflame with scarlet geraniums.

"In the name of the bee/ And of the butterfly/ And of the breeze, amen!" Emily Dickinson's benediction lies upon the flowering curvilinear beds, which flank the bandstand. Crown imperials, daffodils, and tulips bloom first, then peonies and Scotch thistles in June, and later perennial sunflowers will bloom along with phlox and rudbeckias. These plants and flowers, arranged in drifts, have a complimentary concentration of colour and variety. They are Victorian watercolours of English country gardens come to life.

A water-baby is one of the many enchanting details of the turn-of-the-century Boer War Memorial Fountain.

A faint dust rises from the path, fragrances of earth, grass—and odours of popcorn. The canteen, the only other noticeable construction besides the bandstand and waterfowl house, does a brisk business in refreshments. By the rare Japanese umbrella

*Jubilee Fountain, also known as "Nymph Fountain," was
erected in 1897 to honour Queen Victoria's Diamond Jubilee.*

These handsome plants, pink Cleome and white Nicotiana,
make up part of the serpentine beds near the Jubilee Fountain.

pine, children are sowing handfuls of popped corn. The white blossoms fall onto the path and ducks gobble them up. Around the bandstand are geometrically designed formal beds. These hold spring hyacinths, tulips, and muscari, which mysteriously vanish in June. Hibiscus bushes and bedding plants suddenly appear in their place, an overnight conjuration.

Across from the gardens, on the Sackville Street side, are five greenhouses open to the public once a year. Here, the staff lovingly care for and prepare the plants, bulbs, and flowers. Thousands of annuals are started each year from seed and bulbs, iresine and a large quantity of fuchsia and santolina from slips and seeds. The tropical plant collection, which includes hibiscus, palms, agaves, aloes, and bird of paradise, overwinter here because of their susceptibility to frost. Dwarf plants are started and nurtured to be embedded in the two rare plant carpetbeds. These plants have contrasting leaf colours and are not permitted to flower. The little plants are then arranged densely in a design to spell out words and annually commemorate special events.

Transplanted each summer from the greenhouse,
these southern imports provide a touch of the exotic.

The serpentine beds are just one of many planting designs employed in the Public Gardens.

It is the bandstand, however, that takes centre stage. Henry Busch, a Halifax architect, designed the ornate wooden structure. The gingerbread decorations, the bright red roof and trimmings of yellow, green, and white are clearly recognizable from outside the gardens. At night, this gazebo glows with floodlights.

On Sunday afternoons the rows of sun-splashed green benches fill up. People lean against the nearby golden elm or sit on the grass under the

weeping mulberry. In the Victorian and Edwardian eras, and during the two world wars, local and visiting regimental bands played patriotic marching music. On the bandstand roof a flag—the red, white, and blue Union Jack—rippled in the breeze. On festive evenings a band might play waltzes while couples danced on the lawn. Today, musicians serenade the audience with old dance tunes and songs from popular musicals. For ecological reasons, dancing on the lawns is no longer permitted. When all is in full bloom in midsummer and the concert begins when bushes radiate their perfume and the air is ambient with goodwill, we surrender to a ritual that has lasted for 150 years.

Inside the gardens, popcorn, ice cream, and soda are the main merchandise. But through the fence we see a busy market. The fence becomes a wall where street artists hang their colours: oils, sketches, watercolours, photographs, jewellery and trinkets, handmade clothes and hats. A fortune teller reads palms; a magician links silver hoops; a young woman plays gypsy tunes on her violin.

> *I sing of brooks, of blossoms, birds, and bowers:*
> *Of April, May, of June, and July-flowers.*
> *I sing of May-poles, Hock-carts, wassails, Wakes,*
> *Of bride-grooms, brides, and of their bridal-cakes."*

—Robert Herrick

The bandstand viewed across Griffin's Pond.

Swans, geese, and ducks are permanent residents of the Public Gardens.

In autumn the green curtain of trees and shrubs that drapes the gardens slowly begins to change colour and texture: gold, flaming reds, copper, burnt sienna. Before they drop, the needles of the Japanese larch turn to a dazzling yellow. The leaves unhook themselves from trees and strew the crushed stone paths. Chestnuts are scattered across the grass; these are "conkers." Pick one up, break open the spiky shell. There is no lovelier nut than this; new-polished, by gently rubbing on the side of your nose, the conker becomes a lustrous dark mahogany. Pollen-smudged bees burrow deep into the throats of the last flowers.

In wet November the gates are locked. Tree trunks are as dark as the cold black iron fence. Against a grey sky, the leaf-barren trees in winter become silhouettes and take on a new beauty and grace. It is then you can see the articulation of the branches. The limbs of the oval-shaped chestnut have a gentle reverse curve that is unique. In a warmer season it carries showy white blossoms; in winter, with its thick branches laden with snow, it becomes an elegant sculpture. After a freezing rain all the trees and bushes in the gardens are sheathed in a glitter of silver ice— beautiful skeletons that rattle in the wind.

Winter provides a reprieve from human visitors.

Now, winter thoughts are far away as the late afternoon sun urges me to seek my favourite retreat, the Soldier's Memorial Fountain. Under the weeping elms by the fountain it is like a cool, moist, green cave. The wych elms, first discovered at Camperdown, Ireland, have drooping branches that have been grafted onto the upright trunk. Sometimes starlings one by one will drop from the low-hanging branches. So effective is this green umbrella that under a light rain shower you can stay dry. But when the rain slants and the wind climbs uphill, scowling and snarling, from the mouth of the harbour, it is time to seek shelter. Nearby coffeehouses on Spring Garden Road become havens in which to sit out a storm.

After a night's rain, and when the sun has yet to break through the overcast, the air is soft, mist rises from the pond, and all the statues seem to come alive. The cherubs riding dolphins bounce in their saddles. The soldier on the memorial fountain, dressed in South African Campaign uniform and holding a rifle, sighs and shifts his weight a little. The statues of Ceres, goddess of agriculture; and Diana, a moon goddess, at the bath; and Flora, goddess of flowers and spring, all blink in the ethereal light.

I settle under the canopy of weeping branches and make notes:

Ginkgo tree: west side of gardens … the name is Chinese, means silver fruit…. Flowers: delicate purple clematis ... explosion of azalea colours … Chinese asters … snapdragons … gladioli … sweet-faced pansies (also called "heart's ease") … splashes of red poppies…. Spindle trees: their slim branches embracing each other, lovingly entwined, locked together until death.

As the evening light fails, I stroll around the pond. Ducks on the lawn, heads tucked under wings. The soft "quonk-quonk" of those in the water still looking for food—black ducks and green-headed mallards. There are predators: hawks have been seen circling above; osprey dive down to the pond to catch fish; gulls prey on ducklings; there are stories of rough men climbing the fence at night to make off with a captured duck.

The lamposts and bandstand light up. Already the moon is crawling up the sky. Through field glasses I moongaze. As I lower the lenses, what looks like a swallow turns out to be a bat. With its small halved umbrella wings, it dips and veers to skim for insects, dark shadow over water.

The statue of Diana, one of three Roman goddessess placed on pedestals in the Public Gardens, the others being Ceres and Flora.

The moonlight sifts through the trees, the blossoms stir, the air loosens, and ducks swim, leaving wrinkles of water in their wake. The gliding swan is white and eerie in this light. Goldfish dimple the water as they feed and leap into the air, shaking out reflections from the lamplight. The pond gently rocks with the continuous movement of creatures.

A whistle blows. The park policeman advances through the dark. "Tweetle-tweet!" We are being herded out of the gardens; it is lockup time. He is efficient. His flashlight sweeps the flowers close to the path. "We shone the headlamps on the rose-walks," Proust wrote, "and the roses looked like beautiful women we had torn from sleep." The policeman waits patiently for the last couple, who take their time, reluctant to surrender the charms of the gardens.

Out through the old iron gates and we are into the swim of neon lights, the rumble of motorcycles and cars with booming stereos, and crowds of whooping pub crawlers. Out into the rumbling beat, the metal and concrete heart of Spring Garden Road. I pluck a cigarette butt from the mouth of a bust of Sir Walter Scott that some carousing joker planted earlier, and throw it away. I cross the street to Victoria Park.

Visually, this side of Spring Garden has been forever marred by the destruction of some architecturally unique Victorian townhouses. Up the street, panels of light shine from highrise condos—not buildings designed to lift the spirit or complement the gardens. The microclimate of the gardens has already been altered by long shadows cast by these structures.

Friends of the Public Gardens, a registered society, petitioned against the highrises, but to no avail. City councils and developers must have their own way it seems. At the time, they envisioned Spring Garden Road akin to Manhattan's Park Avenue. In New York, at the turn of the century, Olmstead witnessed similar changes during his lifetime—tall buildings and later, skyscrapers all around Central Park, which he helped to create—and he grieved, deeply.

Facing the street is the tall Robbie Burns statue. This is where the Sally Ann operates on some evenings. With their music and message they draw a straggle of people, some of them looking for and finding salvation of one kind or another.

Above me, Burns the poetic Scot, with folded arms stands gazing pensively at the the gardens. You can enjoy the quiet intimacy, the peacefulness of the gardens by yourself, or share it with strangers who arrive from all over the world to walk the paths: peripatetic sailors from distant ports; Americans and Japanese with their small portable video cameras; bus tour travellers from all North American points; British Royalty; and street people. There is no visible sign, the Public Gardens send their own message: "Whoever you are, whatever you do, you are welcome here." And in these Public Gardens is the ineffable sweetness of the true heart of the city.

Indian summer; soon the leaves will unhook themselves from trees and strew the crushed stone paths with gold and bronze and ochre.

*This sandy beach below the Dingle Tower
provides a cool retreat on hot summer days.*

FLEMING PARK

This is Fleming Park. I love the place and spend endless hours idling here, in all seasons. The trails are just the right length, I never tire; and at all times there are fresh, healthy wonders to delight the eyes, the ears, and a twitching nose! There are always people enjoying this demi-paradise, but many, many hidden nooks where I can dream and dwell on the remarkable life of Sandford Fleming. There is no doubt that he loved Halifax, and here is the old stone gate to his estate where, though green with verdigris, the plaque tells every passerby that this is Fleming Glen, where he lived in contented old age.

Once upon a time, a witty dinner speaker said you could turn over a stone anywhere in the world and there would be a Scottish engineer under it. Maybe so. In any event, these stones in this magical glen speak of Sandford Fleming, who landed in Quebec City in 1845 and felt he had gone to a foreign country. As a government surveyor and Chief Engineer for the new Dominion in 1867, he travelled from one end of Canada to the other and chose Halifax as his abiding place. This city was very like his own hometown of Kirkaldy, where a bustling port called the "Lang Toun" stretched out along the shore. He approved of the plain, no-nonsense people like his own. In Kirkaldy, if someone innocently pronounced the "l" he was instantly seized upon as a stranger and set right at once.

Fleming liked the hills and glens surrounding Halifax and most of all those around the Northwest Arm, that tidal inlet so like the myriad lochs, or loughs, of Scotland. He promptly bought a large portion of this territory, planted his staff, and decided he was home. It is our great good fortune that in 1908 he granted 95 acres of this unspoiled beauty to Halifax for all time. I love to remember this wonderfully generous man—the amiable spirit of the park.

A mere ten-minute drive from downtown, in summer, visitors can hike the trails; in winter, the park is open to snowshoers and cross-country skiers. These paths lead to the Dingle Tower, formally called Halifax Memorial Tower, and four distinct natural habitats. In all seasons, there are "gatherings of people." Sandford Fleming would be pleased.

Once through the stone gate the Dingle Road swerves left and leads past the Loop Road Walk to the tower and parking area. The name "dingle," according to Fleming, probably came from the well-known district of that name in Ireland, near Bantry. Dingle, meaning "a deep dell, shaded with trees; a dell is a small wooded hollow or valley." The beach area near the tower was once called "Fairy Cove." Dingle, dell, Irish fairy glen—all words that carry Celtic overtones of mist and mystery. Magic it was to Fleming when he first bought this land as a summer retreat and

built his home. Even though residential areas can be seen through the foliage here and there, today it remains a park of great charm and natural beauty.

Where the Loop Road Walk begins, the ground is sparsely covered with stunted shrubs. Soon the outcroppings of rock give way to lofty pine, poplar, yellow birch, spruce, red maple, and delicate birches that Lucy Maud Montgomery always called "White Ladies." On my earlier spring visits, songbirds practiced courting calls. Black-capped chickadees foraged for food. Funereal crows flew through the trees, cawing loudly. On one side of the path, blue-white patches of snow lingered under the shade of the hemlock trees; on the other, warmed by the sun, last year's leaves curled among the gnarled roots. Every willow bough carried a litter of young "pussies"; children gathered them by the armful. The clear, cold, pale sunlight streamed into the forest.

*A spring mosaic of white birch, flowering red maple,
and mature evergreens along the Seawall Walkway.*

*Opposite page: Bronze lions—their "saddles" polished
and worn through the years by many who posed for
photographs—are quiet sentinels of the Dingle Tower.*

The Loop Walk continues, and around the first bend a winding path leads up to the lookoff. Three young men with backpacks came down the trail. On the rather barren summit are a few trembling aspen and some birch. I sat next to a cluster of young grey birch; their chalky-white trunks and darker delicate limbs and twigs above me were splayed against the sky. This is a place to read, to meditate, or to simply enjoy the long, wide vista of the Northwest Arm.

A silent flutter of colour. I followed the brown wings trimmed in white. The butterfly settled on a bush, then flitted away and was gone; their lives, so brief, so very beautiful. Here, the ground cover is varied: teaberry, mayflower, lambkill, blueberry, bracken, bayberry, cinnamon fern, and huckleberry. In autumn, the huckleberry leaves turn bright red and set the hill on fire. As always, brilliant leaves: scarlet from the maple, shades of yellow from the aspen, poplar, and birch. The bright, dead leaves flutter to the ground—rich humus to support forest life.

In autumn the heath barren, overlooking the North West Arm near the look-off, turns a bright crimson.

*Near the Frog Pond, young woodland
trees show their flares of autumn colours.*

*Sunset and sails on the North West Arm; this inlet has been
a haven to sailors, canoeists, and boaters for over a century.*

"O, pick not our provincial beauties, dear visitor!" That Victorian plea came to me as I perused the Nova Scotian Nature Map, which sounds an alarm about the mayflower. Also called trailing arbutus, it is our provincial flower and the first wildflower to bloom in spring. The map tells us that "it is so eagerly gathered that there is concern for its survival." Picking loosens the roots, so I kneel down and inhale the pale, pink, sweet-smelling blossoms hidden under the leaves. An "evergreen" plant, in age the leaves take on a leathery, rusty appearance.

Now, it is summer, and I am on another visit. Weeds, wildflowers, bushes, and trees in their dense foliage flourish under the extravagant light of the sky. The thick green of the sloping hills dissolves into the blue of the water. On the lookoff I sit by the young grey birch again, green with foliage now, and look up to the aspens with their two-toned leaves— shiny dark green above, yellow green below—quivering in the slightest breeze. All nature makes me dozy in the dreamy summer heat.

Fleming chose well and I imagine him pausing here just long enough to take in the sweep of the Arm dotted with white sails. I say "pause," for here was a man of vast accomplishments, enormous energy, and a vivid imagination, always on the move. He lived in an era when Scots were "engineers to the world," and he became one of the foremost railway engineers of his time. In 1871 he was Chief Engineer of the Canadian Pacific Railway, which spanned the continent. Fleming loved his adopted country and embraced it fully by leading an active life and chalking up honours of which he had never dreamed. In 1897 he became Sir Sandford Fleming. The knighthood was bestowed on him by Queen Victoria.

I follow the Fleming Pathway to the spot where he once had his summer cottage and stable. Only the stable remains, a Heritage Building of ironstone and granite. The grounds are now used to store park benches and gravel for the paths.

What would the Flemings have seen when they ventured out of their cottage in the morning? Outside, the air would have been brisk and sweet. Sir Sandford and Lady Fleming (her name was Jean) would have been greeted by chattering red squirrels, noisy crows, the metallic piping of bluejays, and yellow-rumped warblers darting out of tree tops to snare flying insects. There were berry patches and wildflowers. Raccoons, snowshoe hares, and other small creatures inhabited the woodlands, as they do today. The Flemings might have heard from the Arm faint sounds of oars squeaking in their locks, the snap of sails, the far off moan of a train whistle. As they enjoyed the outdoors, Sir Sandford might have had his bowl of porridge topped with his favourite—marmalade. This was home to Sir Sandford and his wife; New Scotland had given them an abiding place.

On the Fleming Pathway I double back toward the Loop Walk, then cut downhill to the shore. This leads to a grove of trees and a glen of grassy knolls. A crowd of people are having a jolly picnic as they watch boats sail by on the shining water. No wonder an American visitor in the 1800s declared that the Northwest Arm was "too prosaic a name for such a heavenly place," and that it was "one of the prettiest nooks that ever gladdened the eye of a tourist." A hundred years later, visitors from all over the world say the same.

Mussel shells are strewn across the grass, dropped by hungry gulls. There is a busy saltwater life in the waters of the Arm; pollock and mackerel make their home here. Osprey, ducks, and cormorants visit frequently; sometimes loons and heron can be seen. The 4-foot tidal range reveals a variety of plants and sea creatures, including starfish and periwinkles, often called "penny-winkles."

Toward the tower, a glen of spruce and hemlock is divided by a rambunctious freshwater brook that spills down from the Frog Pond to tumble and plunge over rocks and into the ocean below. The Seawall Walk continues along the sandy cove to curve around a headland. The Arm, especially this part of Fleming Park, is a much-loved recreation spot. Until the early 1960s, there was a ferry service across the water of the Arm. The headland, wrote John W. Regan, "leaves the shore at right angles like a flying buttress ... and at its extremity rises to a lovely knoll of 90 feet." This was a natural setting for Sir Sandford's dream to have a memorial tower built within the park. This commemorates the 150th anniversary of the first meeting of an elected government in Canada in 1758.

This was constructed of native granite and ironstone and rises 200 feet in the air. It was officially opened by the Duke and Duchess of Connaught on August 14, 1912. Sir Sandford, with a crown of white hair

Overleaf: Yellow pond lillies decorate the Frog Pond in midsummer. Granite boulders, scattered about the pond, are called "erratics."

Right: Pickerelweed veils the Frog Pond shore with its stiff blue-violet flower spikes rising out of the shallow water.

A metallic-green damselfly rests on bittersweet nightshade.

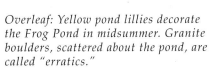

and a bushy beard, was eighty-five years old when he took part in the ceremony. There were fire boats, rockets, flares, illumination by electricity, and massed children's choirs. Two years later, Fleming, the ardent imperialist and father of standard time, died peacefully in Halifax.

I watch as some youngsters ride in the well-worn "saddles" of the two huge bronze lions in front of the tower. Tower and lions: sturdy symbols for the British Empire as it was before the outbreak of World War I. I follow the children and their parents into the tower; the youngsters shout and holler to hear their echoes in the massive structure with its dimly lit interior. The walls hold plaques and panels in native stone from all over the world, contributed by provinces and universities of Canada, by chief cities in Britain, and various dominions and colonies of the Empire. The children are more interested in climbing a spiral staircase and so are the adults after reading all that history written on stone, much of it faded with the years. We all clatter up to the cupola, from which one sees the Northwest Arm, the long inlet of the sea which loses itself far off in the misty Atlantic.

From the tower, on the playground side, is a paved road that leads to a small ironstone and granite church that served the little village at the turn of the century. Today it is used as an ecology and recreation centre. I take the Crossland Ice Trail behind the church. It winds its way up a rocky path and into a wooded area. Through the canopy of trees, a modern vapour trail, a plume of white crosses the sky. Boulders and rocks are everywhere, and noisy children are playing among them. These are "erratics," rocks fragmented by the Ice Age and left to be weatherbeaten, carved by wind, ice, and rain. They are strewn about like cooling loaves from the bread oven. Many are huge, some pointed, some round, some nestled in groups, others alone and brooding; all of them sculptures. Some of the rock ledges are sprinkled with pine needles. Most of the rock surfaces are plated with sheets of lichen. To the children, lichen makes lovely crunchy sounds as they rock jump from one to another. These lichens have a delicate beauty and appear in a fine array of colours and shapes. The most common types in the park are probably shield lichen, with their flat, large, white to grey rosettes decorating trees and rocks, and wall lichen, which, when wet, turns orange rosettes into yellow green.

A mature birch thrives in a groomed, open area along the Seawall Walk;
Lucy Maud Montgomery called these dainty trees, "White Ladies."

Further on there is a running stream shaded by an ancient hemlock. Here are blue-purple flowers of the vinelike nightshade, which carries berries that start green and later change to brilliant red. On the boardwalk, which spans a marsh, two people have set up a tripod and are taking photographs of nature. Black ducks and mallards are paddling and dunking and feeding as they thread through the yellow pond lilies and broadleaved cattails, which are often mistakenly called bullrushes. A woman sketches a swamp rose that grows tall here, from 1 foot to 5 feet. This spectacular flower bursts into bloom in late summer with large, pink hollyhock-like blossoms. Near the swamp rose one day, I saw damselflies mating in the air, their thin bodies green and translucent in the sun. Hermit thrushes are busy looking for insects along wet marshy ground, flicking their rusty tails. The musical piping and reedy tremolos of these birds have been described as "the most beautiful of any North American bird."

The Frog Pond is completely encircled by the trail. Here and there little paths run down to the water's edge. The ruby-crowned kinglet can be seen in the trees. This tiny wing-flicking bird chatters away and sings amazingly loud for such a small creature.

I sit down on one of the benches to watch the gulls standing still like white soldiers on the large grey-blue erratics that push up through the water. The pond, trimmed with trees and foliage, is large enough to be considered a small lake. I think of Coleridge's lines about another pastoral haven: "Here be woods as green as any, air likewise as fresh and sweet … with flow'rs as many as the young spring gives … here be all new delights, cool streams and wells … caves and dells…." Yes, acres of dells; as for caves, well, the dank and stony tower will do nicely.

When the pond is frozen over it is delightfully romantic and especially alluring under moonlight, as all secluded ponds in winter are in Nova Scotia. The thick ice surface of the pond quickly fills with skaters dressed in bright colours. Youngsters bang a hockey puck back and forth, exhilarated by cold air and open space.

But this is summertime. A sweating jogger puffs by as I get up and follow the path. Two women walking their dogs exchange pleasantries with me before they go on. Thoreau once wrote: "A slight sound at evening

*The fondest memories of hockey players usually begin
at a place like this; ice hockey on the Frog Pond.*

lifts me up by the ears, and makes life inexpressibly serene and grand. It may be in Uranus, or it may be in the shutter." Or it may be the sound in the marsh adjacent to the Frog Pond. One evening, under a frond of stars, I heard hundreds of Northern spring peepers, their swelling, high thin chorus ringing out so vibrantly that I was unable to tear myself away from their music. In the spring, the peeper frogs, along with wood frogs, American toads, and yellow spotted salamanders, make their way to the Frog Pond to lay their eggs. Catfish, trout, sticklebacks, minnows, and green and pickerel frogs live in the pond. Hooded mergansers occasionally visit here. It is also home to a pair of beavers. Unbeknown to them,

these hard-working animals stand as an appropriate tribute to Sir Sandford Fleming, who designed Canada's first postage stamp in 1857—a three-penny stamp with the picture of a beaver in a stream of running water. The beaver became, under Fleming's direction, the official symbol of the great Canadian Pacific Railway.

I wander along the path where pickerel weed veils the shore with its stiff, blue-violet flower spikes rising out of shallow water. The late afternoon light begins to ebb; dusk is coming. Pond lilies—all day in the sun, floating among their shining pads—will soon close into tight, round buds of yellow.

At the end of the Frog Pond, near the parking lot, a couple with their daughter are feeding the ducks as I approach.

"What a beautiful evening!" the mother remarks. We all look up at the parcels of cumulus clouds with dark underbellies, packing themselves away. The setting sun is reflected on the cloud tops in hues of mauve, rose, and bright cream—an edible sky. The family of three get into their car and give a cheery wave as they drive off. This is a friendly park.

In the spread of the early evening, people emerge from the park to head home. The ducks are swimming about, still looking for bread; the squawking gulls are not far behind them; and pigeons on shore are picking up the last of the crumbs. Above, the clouds are full of light.

The persuasion of the paths; on the Crossland Ice Trail, woodland paths lead away from the Frog Pond to connect with other pathways.

The romance of Prince Edward and Julie in the 1790s lives on;
years later, the original oval pond was altered to this heart shape.

HEMLOCK RAVINE

L ong before the thin, shiny, dark twigs of red maples flower with tufts of rosy bloom, the brook that runs deep into the ravine is sheeted with ice. One can hear the water gurgling beneath the translucent glassy surface. Into air pockets the dark and lively water swirls and writhes, struggling to break through here and there, impatient with its frozen roof. There is the clarity and music of water running under the ice and one can sense the rush of energy, the reckless and swift-flowing rush. "Heaven is under our feet as well as over our heads," wrote Thoreau as he looked into the hole he had made in the ice at Walden Pond and marvelled at the "softened light and quiet parlour of the fishes."

Heaven, for Prince Edward the Duke of Kent, when he arrived in Halifax in 1794, was the diversion of streams in the ravine to assist in creating a romantic estate of man-made waterfalls, duck houses, temples, and pagodas, landscaped gardens, serpentine walks, enticing arbours, summer houses, secret grottos, and a large, oval-shaped pond known as Julie's Pond.

To complement and share this idyllic retreat—loaned to him by Lieutenant Governor Wentworth—the red-headed bachelor duke brought along his companion, Julie St. Laurent. Her real name was Thérèse-Bernardine Mongenet, a beautiful, dignified, and fashionable French woman, who had served as mistress to two French noblemen. Everyone knew her as Julie and believed that she was a "widowed noblewoman." She and Edward spent six years at what became known as the Prince's Lodge. Servants, gardeners, cooks, and labourers were hired. The prince, as commander of the Nova Scotian forces, had barracks constructed along the Bedford Basin shore to house two companies of his regiment, some of whom were musicians. Julie and Edward became the toast of the town, attending Halifax theatres, and holding balls, soirees, and concerts at their spectacular country getaway. Guests were invited to picnic down by the shore of Bedford Basin and stroll in what we now call Hemlock Ravine.

Although some of the hemlock trees are 250 to 350 years old, this 200-acre site is the "junior" of these four parks, receiving provincial approval as recently as 1983. The natural environment of the ravine has been retained, including a substantial buffer area. Hemlock Ravine is about twenty minutes from downtown Halifax by car or bus. Along the Bedford Basin, past Mount Saint Vincent University, the green-domed roof of the historic music pavilion, a rotunda, and all that remains of Prince's Lodge can be seen on the right, on a knoll close to the water. A turn to the left to the end of Kent Avenue and left again into a small parking lot leads to the ravine park. No iron gates or stone entrances here. There is Julie's Pond, now heart-shaped. It was once rimmed prettily with rocks but now wears a stiff collar of cement.

In Edward and Julie's time, the pond was probably twice as large. Skating parties were held here in the winter. Officers and their guests bundled up in furs and made the pleasurable sleigh ride from Halifax, harness bells jingling and horses bedecked with plumes. The pond is still used in winter; skaters trip over frozen branches poking out of the ice, thrown into the shallow water by youngsters during the summer. The paths and trails are used by cross-country skiers, snowshoers, and hikers.

Spring peepers and salamanders live in the pond, which is also home to a muskrat. A recent addition is a small school of goldfish not indigenous to the pond. These one-time pets shine orange gold through the water and are very pretty, but they pose a threat to the salamander and frog life by feeding on their eggs.

It was early springtime when I waxed lyrical over the ice-topped stream. It is almost summer now; another trip, early June. Along Lady Wentworth Walk the pines and hemlocks thin out to give way to birches, alders, and beeches. The beech is a lovely tree—straight and erect with clean, smooth, light blue-grey bark—and is rarely mistaken for any other tree. Unfortunately, some of them suffer from blight and are twisted and

Mushrooms, moss, ferns, and fallen leaves mingle
on the forest floor along the top of the ravine.

*A bog situated by Lady Wentworth Walk collects rainwater
and promotes the growth of mosses and ferns.*

gnarly, yet there is a certain kind of beauty that exists, even in this form. Their leaves, bright golden brown, remain all winter.

Now and then cyclists pass me on the trail. Where the path fords deep hollows, huge granite blocks fortify its sides; these are believed to have been transported from the Hollis Street waterfront in Halifax. Along the path are wintergreen plants. Gently I pluck one of the thick, slightly-ridged, shiny leaves and press it between finger and thumb—the fragrance is refreshing. The small egg-shaped flowers dangle like little bells beneath the leaves; its fruit is a small, scented red berry.

Of a sudden—there! ... All in blue, joining me on the path ... and my heart quickens. A butterfly is irresistible at any time. Immediately I feel a peculiar tenderness towards this one; the sweetness of its flutter perhaps, its delicacy and vulnerability, certainly its colour. It settles on some moss near the path. I sprawl on the gravel to get within a foot of its colour. I make notes: "underwings greyish ... patterns of small dark spots." I feel like Nabokov, writer and lepidopterist; however, he had a green net to catch his prize and was an expert on butterflies, which, alas!, he impaled on pins. A couple walks past, stares, and politely moves on. The "blue" is gone, but there are other "blues" as I continue my hike. These endearing creatures are called Spring Azure, and when they are out, you know that summer will soon officially arrive. Except for the sky, blue is the rarest colour in nature. And nature sweetens the mind, for now I feel rejuvenated.

> "The earth lies out now like a leopard, drying her lichen and moss spotted skin in the sun, her sleek and variegated hide."
> —Thoreau

Somewhere around the Wentworth Loop I find myself moving toward large boulders and stretches of clifflike rocks. This long rock wall is covered with a variety of lichens. How beautiful are the colours, soft grey-mauve with dark violet-brown bubbles. The wall's terrain is like the surface of the moon. When wet it turns shades of light brown with faint streaks of pink and greeny yellow; litmus paper is made from an extract of lichens. I press my hand, carefully and gently, on the delicate carpet of parchmentlike growth. They are the only plants, nature writer Roger Caras tells us, that can grow on otherwise barren rocks and are, in fact, "one of the principal means by which rocks are decayed and turned to soil."

The confusion of the main paths! There are times I know not where I am in this pleasant maze, perhaps on the Prince Edward Path, or possibly on the Sir John Wentworth Loop, which passes Friar Lawrence Way and later meets Lady Wentworth Walk, which in turn crosses the Governor Trail, and so on. Frustrating, perhaps because each path runs in a circle. However, as Shakespeare said, "It's all one!" So I pack away my map and elect to saunter off the main trails and follow my nose and eyes wherever they choose to go.

The animal trails I follow lead to moss-covered boulders, soft and velvety to the touch, with a strong smell of damp moss around a large hemlock tree. Its hide is a deeply furrowed, reddish-brown bark. Under the hemlock I look up to see its branches curve; it has grown in a slight arc, bent by prevailing winds, its fan of needles against blue sky. The needles, really leaves, have distinguishing features: they are blunt-pointed and flat, grow in two ranks, and each is attached to the side of the twig by a threadlike stalk. This is the only eastern coniferous species with a stalked leaf. The roots are deep, and according to Caras the hemlock is "an ultimate tree, unadorned by climbers or runners or busy growth."

Further on are roots and green foliage dappled by the sun; I am into the cool of shaded mossy dells. Underfoot, the sphagnum moss is a thick, rich, springy carpet, damp in the shade. Little fungus plants thrive in the genial dampness. There are holes and burrows everywhere, homes perhaps for small creatures. Crows control the upper register of trees and let strangers know it. These crows roost by the thousands in a group of tall trees just behind the grounds of Mount Saint Vincent.

Deep in the woods, through tangles of bushes and branches, I find a comfortable spot, a mossy rock that serves as a bench. Sunlight filters through the trees. A breeze brings the tang of spruce, maple, and oak; green summer has risen in all the parks. I wait and watch and listen, quietly eating my lunch. Anchored between two pines, a single thread of spider silk vibrates and flashes in the light. There is the susurration of the wind through branches, a whispering.

It is as though my arrival has been approved, for all at once birdsongs

Along the Wentworth Loop, birch trees present a creamy-white backdrop for a sturdy Northern red oak and a white pine.

begin. All around me, coming from trees, from the ground, from the air:
bluejays, robins, a red-eyed vireo, chickadees, a Canada warbler, and a
song sparrow with its short notes, then a trill, sometimes interpreted as,
"Madge-Madge-Madge, put-on-your-tea-kettle-ettle-ettle." A sharp tap-
tap from a downy woodpecker working its way around a birch tree, its
white-spotted black wings easily seen from my rocky perch. The dark
shape of a crow floats low through the trees. There is nothing to fear here.
Small harmless animals inhabit the woodlands. There are white ermine
in winter, deer wander through the park and love to visit nearby gardens
to gorge on tender new tulips, and the usual little creatures such as cheeky
squirrels, field mice, and voles. "True solitude," wrote Edward Hoagland,
"is a din of birdsong, seething leaves, whirling colours, or a clamour of
tracks in the snow."

The right fork of the Governor Trail leads down into the ravine. The
trail here is rocky, wet in places, and woven with tangles of roots. It was
once used as an old coach road in Edward and Julie's time. The stream

*The hobblebush, so named because its branches often root where they touch
the earth, blooms with clusters of white hydrangea-like flowers in spring.*

*Cinnamon ferns—which have nutty-flavoured edible stem
cores—show their rusty curls in damp, wooded areas.*

was full-flowing then and provided fresh, clear drinking water. The early spring rush over, it now runs like a tranquil brook. In sunlight the mossy stones in the water become a radiant green. On the steep, sloping bank is a virgin stand of hemlocks, offering their wealth of years to the sky.

In winter, snowflakes become trapped in the canopy of the hemlocks. The branches hold melted snow and rain water, to become gushing waterspouts during the spring. On a drizzly day, it seems primordial here

Their branches topped with fresh snow, noble hemlocks hold the wealth of their years to the sky.

with curls of mist rising from the brook and the trees. Hanging in the air is a pungent smell of woods, fungus, and bog. Light rain stipples the pools of water. On a wild day the wind seethes through the hemlocks; the trees are moaning and keening. Now and then an ancient, noble hemlock will come crashing down the slope. Of all the parks, the ravine is the least landscaped; nature is left to practice its own refinement. The old hemlock will rest where it falls to become host to a vast array of fungus, then total decay—fertile earth for new hemlocks.

In the ravine by the brook it is peaceful. Sitting on a log I see across the stream, glossy birches against dark evergreens. I stroll by the stream to look for plant life, water bugs, or perhaps animal tracks, or simply watch the quality of light change throughout the afternoon.

Sturdy boots are required in order to continue, for soon the trail diminishes to become a rough and narrow footpath with rocky outcroppings. Branches clutch at my sleeve as I pause to make notes: "small, delicate, white Indian pipe plant ... cinnamon fern, sometimes called Indian meat for its nutty-flavoured edible stem core ... hobblebush flowers ... mushrooms." The steep bank levels off and soon there is the smell and sound of cars; the trail, for a short distance, runs somewhat close to a highway. My feet are weary from hours of hiking and I stumble about, threading through birch and beech trees to open sunny patches and scattered boulders.

The traffic noises from the upper highway are well behind me now and a cooling wind picks up. I look back to the crowns of white pines and swaying tips of tall hemlocks. Ahead, creamy white birch trees streaked with sun. Clinging to a dead branch—diaphanous, curled, and glowing with light—one last year's leaf, quivering.

A visitor may become visually saturated with all the green foliage, but there are bright points of colour. In season there is the autumn crimson of Canada's emblem, the red maple. And there are "flowers wild, and sweet." One of the colourful blooms is the pink Lady's-slipper, a flower that should not be picked or disturbed. It is sometimes called moccasin-flower because of its heavily veined, deeply cleft pink pouch. Another beauty that cries out to be left alone is the Painted Trillium. This is an exquisite flower with white petals and at its heart, a red blaze.

On a bench at the fork of two paths is seated a retired couple from Saskatchewan. We strike up a conversation; they are good-humoured and keen on parks. They plan to return next year to explore the Cabot Trail in Cape Breton. In late September, I tell them, it is the most beautiful place to be in North America. "Ahh," they say together, eyes wide open, looking longingly into the distance. Then they ask about the rotunda on the

Bedford Basin shore. Is it open for visitors? Unfortunately no, I tell them, and explain that it now belongs to the province; caretakers live in the building. When the railroad came through in the last century, the promontory on which the rotunda was built was divided. It is dangerous even for service vehicles to enter the grounds because of the train traffic.

The building, the only remaining structure from the romantic days of Edward and Julie, reflects an eighteenth-century Georgian aristocratic passion in England for temples, heart-shaped lakes, and various garden "follies." At one time the interior of the dome was painted blue with white stars. The rotunda is still there for us to admire—unfortunately, mostly from the roadside—and to imagine the music concerts with the famous couple in attendance.

The relationship between Edward and Julie lasted twenty-seven years. Because of a need for an heir to the throne, Edward married a German princess; he fathered a daughter, who became Queen Victoria. Julie lived out her remaining years in Paris, alone by choice.

After bidding goodbye to the friendly visitors, I walk down to the Bedford Basin to wait for a bus. Even the swish of rushing traffic cannot erase the images of a visit to the ravine. I will carry them home with me, along with scales of pine cone clinging to my jacket, bits of lichen crackling in my pockets, pine pitch like glue on my fingers. Just before the bus

The rotunda, with its blue domed ceiling painted with white stars, was built by Prince Edward and his mistress Julie, and hosted numerous musical concerts in the 1790s.

Opposite page: Members of the Rockingham Heritage Society dress up in 18th century costumes for the annual Duke of Kent's Tea held at Julie's Pond.

The Painted Trillium, a member of the
lily family, is an endangered species.

pulls up, I look across at the rotunda. In the late afternoon sun, the surrounding trees throw long and lovely shadows.

Later, the upper branches of the hemlocks will catch the last of the evening light. Hikers will look up to the fringe of trees against the sky. They will hear a rustling in the darkening woods—an owl? bat?— and they will quicken their pace. A loon will fly over the forest sounding its haunting call. Soon, the moonlight will begin to seep into the piney darkness. Deep in the hush of the ravine the moon will dip into the running brook.

"Only that day dawns to which we are awake," wrote Thoreau. "There is more day to dawn. The sun is but a morning star." As the park begins to kindle into life again, an early walker at dawn will catch a brief flash of a deer. Birds will twitter and preen in the branches. The wind will sweep up from the Bedford Basin, and all the green will tremble. The morning will be burnished with a sense of wonder.

In early spring the bronze foliage of the Indian Pear bush shines out, and then entire hillsides are white with its blossoms in May.

*Sunset on the North West Arm; visitors on trails and
sailors on water think of heading home, and into port.*

POINT PLEASANT PARK

Point Pleasant Park, close to downtown Halifax, is often the first large park that visitors experience. Permanent residents come to love this seaside sanctuary, just as I have over the years; the park is like a dear old friend. This sea-girt forest—with its cannons and forts built by the British in the late 1700s as a defence against possible French invasion and still in place—was transformed into a sylvan retreat for the public in 1872. At that time Major-General Horace Montagu of the Royal Engineers laid out the broad carriage drives, the serpentine roads, and the bridle paths and foot trails of Point Pleasant. In the last century, 186 acres of forest were leased to the city for 999 years, at a nominal rent of one shilling per year. This is always paid. There were no automobiles at the time, but one could walk or travel by carriage along Pleasant Street and over Freshwater Bridge at the foot of Inglis Street, which led to what is now the Shore Road entrance.

The most commonly used approaches today are South Park Street and Tower Road; both lead to the park from the heart of the city—a good twenty-minute walk. Tower Road takes the visitor directly to an entrance with stone walls and gates, which at night are lighted by cast-iron street lamps made in 1900 in Glasgow. South Park Street becomes Young Avenue and arrives at what was once the main entrance, where the original heavy antique "golden gates" still stand, somewhat tarnished now but intact and folded back on their hinges. Straight ahead is a flowing fountain, and on the right, the park keeper's "rough-faced" stone house, completed in 1896.

Quarry Pond, a slate quarry that formerly produced building stones, now presents a Monet picture of peaceful waterlilies.

Colonel Cornwallis, sent to establish a fortified town in the 1700s, which became Halifax, saw "the Point" through a "soldier's eye." Today, we look with hiker's eyes, out to the open sea through tall trees. Whatever path, walk, or trail one chooses, serendipity awaits. To loiter, means to linger, to saunter, and so we do, enticed by the salt air.

The first saunter may be along the Shore Road by the ocean. It is a radiant morning, warm enough but with a cool breeze. Runners glow with health, and walkers clip by with their odd exaggerated arm action. On this exhilarating day I experience wanderlust and feel eager and curious to move out and embrace everything around me. A crowd of noisy young people, released from the confines of school for the summer, eyes and faces bright and alive to the unfolding of the day, rush by. Their vitality hums in the air.

A splendid variety of trees border the road. In sunlight the bark of the Scots pine glows reddish-brown; in shadow it takes on a verdigris hue. Its branch tips curve upright to stand like candles. There are a few elegant Austrian pine that stand erect with a majestic air. Thin, tall black spruce wear top-heavy crowns. Flowering shrubs and hardwoods shed their petals, which strew the paths like confetti. Trembling aspens give the illusion that, in the brisk breeze, each leaf is revolving 360 degrees. Someone once said: "It is an unfortunate man or woman who has never loved a tree." The people of Halifax are fortunate; the parks are full of trees, lovingly tended.

In a pleasant clearing, a friendly picnic table beckons with carved messages on its surface, a romantic "OUR SPOT." It is mine and the squirrels' now as they fight over crumbs from my midmorning snack. In my notebook I scribble: "curled dock grows here … wild radish, too … Queen Anne's lace ... and an enormous pile of open and broken mussel shells under a tree, which gives an image of dozens of rambunctious seagulls enjoying a banquet." From the corner of my eye the tawny-red forest floor ripples like a wave; it is those pert and pesky squirrels—almost the same colour, three of them now—on a tear around the trees. Even jays and crows seem tamer here than in other parks.

A right turn up Prince of Wales Drive and I plunge directly into the forest to be in the heart of the park. The park attendants have been at

Black Rock Beach, with its protective slate bedrock, has always lured summer swimmers; "Polar Bear Club" members dip and shiver on New Year's Day.

work; throughout the woodland there is selective cutting of damaged trees to allow new growth to establish itself under the existing forest. The result is numerous shorn stumps and an abundant scattering of wood chips here and there, which gleam in the light and give off a pleasant scent. The hollowed centre of a decaying tree stump has filled up with a growth of moss and fungi, dusted with a layer of broken pine cones. Nestled close is a young pine with plump needle tips, its branches spread like a fan. Around the base of the stump is a ring of bright green moss. Sprinkled about on the earth below is a form of moss and fungi, flowerlike, with slim, curving, dark brown stems and pale, pale faces; as Alden Nowlan would call them, "reticent and subtle ... full of tremulous loveliness." The overall effect is one of a miniature Japanese garden, and there are many of these tiny gardens in the forest.

Here and there springs bubble out of the earth and slow moving streams are fringed with moss. Quiet ponds reflect the trees and sky. Frederick Law Olmstead, a famous park designer, once wrote: "It does men and women good to come together in this way in pure air and under the light of heaven." People love to wander here. Dogs, too! These small pools of water are jolly playgrounds for canines; like children, they wade in to muck about and splash, provoking the most alarming shouts of "Come here!" from their owners.

The forest opens up onto a sumptuous spread of heather. This is one of the very few wild heather patches in North America. Its origin is more than likely the eighteenth century, when a Scottish regiment, probably the Black Watch, brought with them heather-stuffed mattresses. Each morning when bedding was shaken out and rolled up, heather seeds spilled out, took root, and grew. In July, the heather patch blooms with pink flowers. It is so serene here that I feel the urge to bring a sleeping bag and spend a night under the stars, but camping, of course, is not allowed. European beech grow along the edges of the heather patch, near Heather Road. I run my hand over the lovely thick bark of these trees that have become a favourite carving surface for those who insist on leaving their mark: initials, dates, hearts, crosses, and even names of entire families—the universal longing for immortality.

Rare and wild are the Scottish heather patches that grow profusely along Heather Road, and close by the Sailor's Memorial.

Cambridge Battery is not far away, and like most of the historic remnants of a fortified past, its ruins now provide a site for picnics, play, and family gatherings. Around the fort site are wild Lily-of-the-valley under apple trees, and a Norway spruce with its drooping branches and soft needles. Along with Fort Ogilvie, its concrete remains are marvelously suited to open-air theatre. The Shakespeare By The Sea company presents the Bard's plays each summer. Conceived and directed with great imagination and enthusiasm from an innovative young company, the productions have been received with affection and acclaim by Haligonians and tourists.

Footpaths through the woods on the other side of Ogilvie Road lead me to Nature Walk. A series of wall-like slate outcroppings are spangled with afternoon light. Witchhazel grows tall in the moist earth of small ravines. Only one species of this tree with astringent bark and leaves grows in Canada, unique because it is our only native tree that flowers in autumn when the leaves are falling, a tangled mass of golden-yellow clusters.

Along Birch Road the tall trees stand with their crowns of slender ascending branches. Birch, white pine, and spruce are everywhere in the park. Wild sarsaparilla grows calf-high, its greenish-white flowers are in bloom and appear shy, hard to see under the shelter of its drooping leaves. In the last century, the roots of this plant were made into a popular beverage and used in patent medicines. Natives used the root for emergency food.

It is a short walk to Pine Road and then down the steep hill to the canteen for refreshment. From there a winding footpath takes me back to a scattering of slate outcroppings. I could spend all day here, canopied by trees, with patches of sunlight and shadow. Flat on my back on a boulder as big as two beds, I close my eyes, adjust the backpack for a pillow, and daydream. The breeze is scent-laden, leaves rustle, and birds sing. There is the sound of voices, and a dog barks far away. It is easy to fall asleep, and I do.... "Caw, caw!" Crows, flapping through the trees, wake me. Dreamy happiness takes over the hours.

Another path looks promising and off I go again. Whither? No matter. It is almost impossible to become lost or lonely here. There is always some-

Above: The ruddy coloured
leaves of the European copper
beech transform as autumn
approaches to dark green, then
change back to copper again.

Northern red oak leaves grow on
branches sturdy enough to hold a
swing or hammock; the tree holds
on to its leaves late into the winter.

one around the bend of a path, coming or going: runners, walkers, cyclists, dogs and their owners, a policeman mounted on a horse or a pair of constables riding bikes, groups of children. One might even meet the "Crowman," a mature gentleman with a walking stick and a shoulderbag of food that he feeds to the crows. They fly from tree to tree, following him. I cross Cambridge Drive and take Cable Road, a pleasant meander down to Arm Road. Around the turn from Cambridge Drive onto Arm Road there stands a magnificent beech tree. As I reach it there is a sound of rushing leaves and beating wings, then—a flash of blue as two jays shoot out of the dense foliage to spin and whirl past within inches of me; they fall in a noisy squawking heap 50 feet away, chase each other, and fly off in different directions. Jays: jokers of the north, light-hearted bullies, but beautiful in radiant blue. This could have happened in any other park; somehow it suits Point Pleasant. Perhaps what excited me

Noisy bluejays love to bury acorns and seeds, most of which are never retrieved; in effect, jays become tree planters!

was the European beech tree with its dark, ruddy-coloured oval leaves, so strongly veined and fringed with tiny hairs, contrasted with the surprise appearance of the blue-and-lavender jays emerging from the deep copper tones of the beech tree.

Every season serves up its delights. Last spring, on a thick and foggy day, I hiked this route. Foghorns groaned out their warnings. People moved like phantoms along the winding paths. Light scattered showers were predicted. Rain began to splatter bare branches and me. Ink ran into smudges on the pages of my notebook. Then, an unpredicted heavy downpour began. I ran up Tower Road hill to the Martello Tower, where I took shelter, hoping the beating rain would let up. Prince Edward, that tireless builder who became commander of all Atlantic forces and was the "romantic" duke of Hemlock Ravine fame, supervised the construction of this two-storey fort with its 8-foot thick ironstone walls. Eight feet! No wonder it was considered impregnable against eighteenth and nineteenth century 6-pounder guns. The smell of gunpowder still seems to cling to the walls and the vaulted ceiling. Four of these round towers were built around Halifax, the first of their kind in the British Empire. Although the spartan interior can hold two hundred men, it is claustrophobic at any time when one is alone. I braved the rain, hurried to the nearest downtown coffeehouse, and purchased hot chocolate.

Each glorious summer day in the park becomes a gift; the season goes too quickly. Then autumn comes, and one enters another kingdom. In late September and early October, Point Pleasant is radiant with colour, flamboyant with autumn hues. Cheeks of children are the colour of apples. People dress in the colour of leaves: russet, dark red, umber, ochre, scarlet. On Sundays, Cambridge Drive is full of people walking the earthy floor, which is carpeted in bronze, and looking up at the bright autumn sky through knotted branches. Bushes are decorated with spun nets of spider silk. Leaves on the trails rustle like mice. Red squirrels are everywhere, collecting the remains of pine cones for their winter pantry. Crows seem blacker than black against the yellow and gold of trees. There is the wind's wild buffeting as the leaves fall, and fall, and fall. Old pine trees, their shaggy manes blown by the wind, moan with age. The ocean is grey blue with whitecaps, and skirling seagulls hang above the rocking waves.

Grooved and glacially buffed, the Chain Rock was named for a chain boom erected across the North West Arm in 1762 to impede enemy ships.

The last sailing races of autumn are taking place. It is a season in which one feels elated and melancholy by turns.

Every season has its charm. Winter snow fills the park with people, their clothes vivid colours of a summer rainbow. The snowy paths and trails are tramped down by cross-country skiers and snowshoers. On a clear and sunny windless day in winter, the park shimmers with beauty. Walking is invigorating, and the snow-laden pine boughs—busy with the traffic of chickadees, jays, and crows—present animated Christmas cards.

Now, another season, described by Anne Wilkinson as, "gentle, simmering June and leaf and love release their sweetest juice." Along Arm Road are grassy nooks and knolls and below, on the gull-haunted rocks, sunbathers picnic, read novels, or watch sails tacking against contrary winds. At the Point, along the shore and across from the summer house, there is the smell of blossoms and ocean. Strong winds and rains may whip the shore here, but bushes and plants thrive on the seaside slope. One of them is the English hawthorn tree, dense and twiggy with long thorns and crooked zigzag branches. In spring its white flowers bloom, and in autumn its fruit is crimson. Triangles of white appear through the branches—sails, a race is on!

What a breathtaking view: the harbour mouth spreads wide to create a vista to the open sea. Years ago, spectators crowded the Point to watch Nova Scotia's famous schooner, the original *Bluenose,* compete in sailing races with New England vessels. The *Bluenose* was unbeatable. The Point was called Sandwich Point in 1749, when Colonel Edward Cornwallis chose it as a site for a town. Rocky shoals and southeast gales made the idea impractical. Cornwallis established a new town site, later called Halifax, two miles up the harbour. The Point has always been alluring, even with the threat of raids back in Cornwallis' time. A redcoat guard was provided for the determined townsfolk who liked their Sunday afternoon walks to the Point. Dressed in their finest, citizens marched to fife and drum between the files of soldiers armed with rifles and bayonets. Each sunny Sabbath, this rather droll and solemn procession made its way toward the pine forest.

Later on, at nightfall, the plangent sounds of the neighbouring container pier and the searing blaze of its bright lights may seem a shocking intrusion to a visitor, who has spent a pastoral day walking the gentle paths in the park. Accustomed to such incongruities, most people today simply ignore it and carry on. In the parking lot by the water's edge, couples in cars will be "watching the submarine races," Haligonian romantic parlance—a place for lovers. In the last century, Kissing Bridge, which spanned the stream at Pleasant Street, served the same purpose and was a favourite haunt of lovers on flirtatious summer evenings beneath

"This most excellent canopy—the air."
—*Hamlet*

Now it is time to double back and head up Fort Road to Fort Ogilvie, where Shakespeare By The Sea is scheduled to perform. Like Cambridge Battery and Martello Tower, Fort Ogilvie is a fine picnic spot with a generous spread of grass, and scattered around are raspberry and blackberry patches. Behind the fort, the earth is laced with trails and footpaths. Some of these may go as far back as the original native trails, for the Mi'kmaq loved this forest. Poking up through the soil are old and rusty wire cables, once laid down the steep slope, past stands of fir and peeling birch, to the shore and into the harbour. This was part of a WW II underwater net to block enemy submarines from entering the harbour. The concrete remains of the fort now serve as a natural theatre. Centre stage, an ancient black cannon points its muzzle out to sea. The fort is rimmed with bigtooth aspens; one has seven long, thick, spreading branches coming out of a sturdy trunk. These are wide and graceful trees, trees you want to climb, branches you want to sit in—all the potential of stage props.

And sit in them the actors did, hang in them too, and sang as they swung from the branches flashing lights and mirrors. From the bowery clefts, the leafy shelves, and the twining paths, more actors came, nymphs and knaves in white. In and over and all around the trees they performed *A Midsummer Night's Dream.* Birds twittered and squirrels scampered in and out of bushes, while leaves rustled in the breeze like applause. Over the forest, the gathering dusk. In this evening light the players became spirits in the wind, the play, magic. As the audience

*Bridle paths located above Shore Road provide
the perfect venue for a romantic stroll.*

dispersed, the sprites in white blinked their lights behind the pillars of trees and down the forest path. "O wonderful, wonderful, and most wonderful wonderful! and yet again wonderful…!"

Into the darkling woods, the cool forest full of sleeping plants, flowers, trees. "Oh, that summer moon!" wrote Basho, "I wandered round the pond all night." Yes, you too, may wander in this park as late as midnight in the summer, and moon watch. When the moonlight brushes the tree tops, it drifts like snow down onto the paths. In the forest the ponds mirror the last glimmer of evening sky.

You may walk with Whitman, "with the tender and growing night, call to the earth and sea half-held by the night," as you hear the whistle buoys faintly sounding in the harbour, and inhale the sweet, resinous scent of the pines.

One of two summer houses, built in 1881; this one at the Point is an invitation for lunch with a view of the ocean.